Sally Ride
Science

Beth Geiger

CLEAN WATER

ROARING BROOK PRESS

NEW YORK

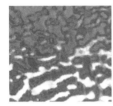

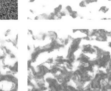

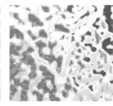

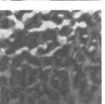
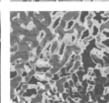

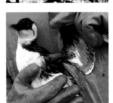

Clean
Water

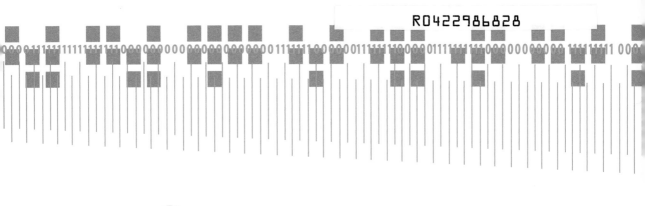

CONTENTS

OUR THIRSTY WORLD

Water is our most precious resource. Every living thing on Earth—every plant, animal, and microbe—must have water to survive. People depend on clean water to drink. We use water every day to wash, to cook, and to grow food. We also use water to make everything from paper to airplanes to cell phones.

Even though much of our planet is covered in sparkling blue water, very little of it is drinkable. Yet, over the years, we've polluted our water with waste, contaminated it with chemicals, and wasted it without thinking. And most serious of all, we've polluted our air with heat-trapping greenhouse gases—especially carbon dioxide—that are affecting Earth's climate. And that is affecting our water supplies, from New York to Beijing and from Cairo to Cape Town.

As the number of people on our planet continues to grow, it gets harder and harder to supply clean, fresh water to everyone. What are we doing about it? A lot! Read on.

In the parched village of Peeplee Ka Bas, India, water wells are dry. Trains haul tankers of water to thirsty villagers who have 15 minutes to fill their buckets every two days.

WATER, WATER, EVERYWHERE

Earth is a watery planet. You'd think we would be up to our necks in clean, drinkable water. But 97 percent of Earth's water is salt water, and we can't drink it. Another two percent is locked up as ice. The rest, just one percent, glistens in our lakes, rushes down our rivers, and hides beneath our soil. That's the water we use—when we can capture it, keep it clean, and get it to where we need it.

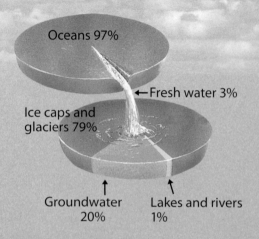

Oceans 97%

←Fresh water 3%

Ice caps and glaciers 79%

Groundwater 20%

Lakes and rivers 1%

Pass the Un-salt

Ever had a gulp of ocean water? Yuck. Your body rejects salt water because it can't absorb that much salt. If you drank a lot of salt water (and didn't lose your lunch trying), your body would try to get rid of the extra salt by urinating. But urine is less salty than salt water, so you would have to urinate more than you drank. You'd lose so much water that you would die of—believe it or not—dehydration.

H₂O—Mighty Molecule

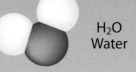

H₂O
Water

Water has a catchy nickname—H₂O. That's its chemical formula. The formula means that every molecule of water is made of two atoms of hydrogen (H) and one atom of oxygen (O). This molecule is a *real* transformer.

- *No other substance exists naturally as a solid, liquid, and gas at temperatures we find here on Earth.* Lucky for us! This makes it possible for water to be recycled from the oceans to the air to the land and through living things—again and again.

- *No other liquid expands when it freezes.* This cool characteristic means that ice is less dense than water. So ice cubes float in your soft drink. And in cold winters, ice floats on the surface of lakes, leaving a watery habitat below for aquatic critters.

Water is sometimes liquid (above), sometimes ice (above, right), sometimes vapor (right). Look around you. What are some examples of water in its three forms?

7

A Walking Bag of Water

That's you! Your body is 60 percent water by weight. It has to be. Every cell in your body needs it. The tiny drop of water inside every cell is where most chemical reactions take place. Water flushes toxins from your system, keeps your organs functioning properly, and even helps you maintain the right body temperature. It's a wonder you don't squish when you walk.

Drink Up!

Every person on the planet needs water. If you don't drink enough, your body can't function well, and you won't feel your best. Most people need about eight glasses of water each day. You've got to keep drinking water to replace the water that constantly leaves your body. You're like a walking sprinkler. Water molecules are flying into the air from all over your body—every time you exhale, sweat, blink, cough, smile, talk, and go to the bathroom. A person can live for weeks without food. But few would survive longer than three days without water. Go ahead, pour yourself a glass.

What's a Liter?

If you drink eight glasses of water today, you'll have guzzled about two liters. A large bathtub holds about 190 liters. An Olympic-sized swimming pool holds approximately 1,000,000 liters of water. Now that's a lot of water.

8

Waterless

Imagine a day without using water. No washing, no flushing, and not much cooking. Sounds pretty dry, doesn't it? In the U.S., every person uses an average of 300 to 380 liters (80 to 100 gallons) of water every day—and that doesn't include the water we drink. That's about two big bathtubs full of water. The biggest water hogs in most homes? Washing and flushing.

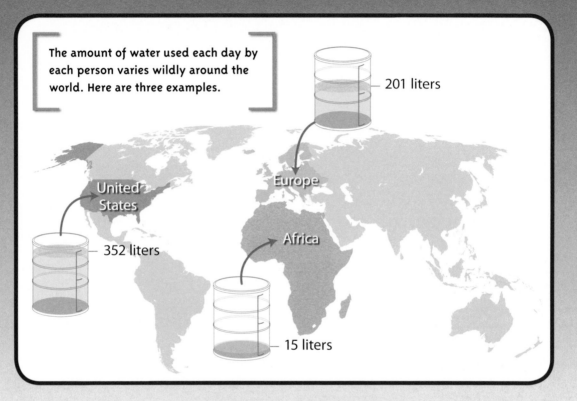

The amount of water used each day by each person varies wildly around the world. Here are three examples.

201 liters

Europe

United States

352 liters

Africa

15 liters

4 u 2 Do

Just a Drop in the Ocean

Fill a clear one-liter bottle with tap water and add some blue food coloring. This bottle represents all the water on Earth. How much of it do you think is drinkable? Remove 30 milliliters (about 2 tablespoons) and drip it into a clear plastic cup. Now the water in the bottle is all the water in our oceans. That teeny amount in the cup? All the fresh water on our planet! Really.

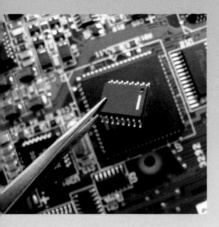

Industrial Strength

Manufacturing is a real supersoaker when it comes to water use. It slurps up 284,000 liters (75,000 gallons) of water to churn out every ton of steel used to make refrigerators, bicycles, ships, and millions of other products. Boiling-hot water makes steam that is used to turn crude oil into chemicals that go into basketballs, sunglasses, and trash bags. Water's also used to clean microchips, which have to be sparkling clean before they go into electronics inside TVs, DVDs, and wireless phones.

Water Wheels

Water's an essential ingredient in many everyday products. It takes 148,000 liters (39,000 gallons) of water just to make one car. Water goes into processing the rubber used to make a car's tires, the steel that forms its body, the glues that hold a lot of it together, and the paint that gives the new ride its shine.

Nothing Dry About This Book

Paper manufacturing is also water intensive—it uses a lot of water. To make paper, wood is squashed to a pulp (bottom, left) and cooked in water to separate out the cellulose (bottom, right). Cellulose is the tough molecule that makes the wood of trees strong. Even more water is used to wash the cellulose further to turn it into a wet sheet of paper. In Duluth, Minnesota, a paper mill uses more than 25 percent of all water used in the city. Now that's a thirsty industry.

Waterlogged

Can you really fit 568 liters (150 gallons) of water into a loaf of bread? That's how much water it takes to grow the grain and other ingredients that go into it. An amazing 40 percent of the fresh water used in the U.S. is used in agriculture—watering the corn, wheat, potatoes, strawberries, and spinach that grow in our fields.

How About a Straw with that Burger?

It takes about 5,000 liters (1,300 gallons) of water to *grow* a hamburger. Farmers grow grains to feed the cows, and the cows drink water, too.

Can That Idea

This will take the fun out of your fizz—far more water goes into making an aluminum soda can than goes into a glass of water. First, water is used to extract aluminum from bauxite ore mined from the ground. And those aluminum cans? Water's used to rinse them over and over before they're labeled and filled with your favorite soft drink.

Water Power

Water is also used to generate power. Rushing rivers can be harnessed to make electricity at dams and hydroelectric power plants. To generate electricity, water is sent rushing over turbines inside a powerhouse at a dam. This makes the turbines spin, generating electricity. Water is also used for cooling at other types of power plants. Much of this water is returned (left) to its source and can be reused. Still, using water to generate electricity puts a strain on water supplies.

> Whoosh! The 17 turbines at Hoover Dam generate electricity for more than 750,000 people.

3

WATER DOESN'T GROW IN BOTTLES

Come to think of it—why is there any water on land at all? The answer is, of course, rain! Or snow!

Water Coaster

When water evaporates from the ocean, the salt is left behind. The water vapor (now fresh water!) is transported through the air, and some of it is carried over land. It eventually drizzles or pours down as rain, or it snows down in flurries or blizzards. Then it's stored in snowpack and lakes, drains into streams and rivers, or seeps into the ground. Yes, it's all water—but if it's on the surface (lakes, rivers, ponds), it's called surface water, and if it's underground, it's called groundwater.

It's All Downhill from Here

No, a watershed is not a new type of raincoat. It's a chunk of land where all the water flows downhill into one river. Think of a watershed as a large funnel. All the rain, melting snow, creeks, streams, lakes, and groundwater in the funnel drain into the same river. Everyone lives in a watershed. Which one do you live in?

Groundwater?

Chances are that not far below your feet, the soil or rock is saturated with water. Water from the surface can seep underground. It fills all the little gaps and cracks—called pores—within sand, soil, and rock. Then it's called groundwater. Hmmm. Why isn't it called *underground water?*

Does This Float Your Boat?

Nope. You can't float your boat in groundwater. It's not like an underground river or lake. Groundwater soaks into the earth, which acts like a big sponge, mopping up the water in all the tiny cracks and crevices.

No Kidding!

There is 100 times more groundwater on Earth than there is fresh water on our planet's surface. Who knew?

A is For Aquifer

An aquifer is an underground reservoir. It can be a meter (3.3 feet) or a kilometer (0.6 miles) below the surface. It can be a meter or hundreds of meters thick. Almost any type of rock or soil can hold water. Some of the biggest aquifers are made of sandstone, which has lots of pores, or spaces, between the sand grains. An aquifer can be as small as an underground schoolyard or so big that it stretches under several states, like the Ogallala Aquifer in the Midwest. Experts say the aquifer has dropped 46 meters (150 feet) because so much water has been drained from it.

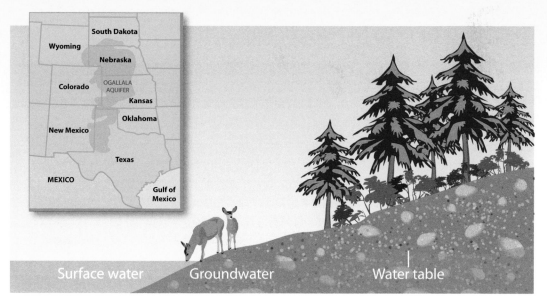

Surface water   Groundwater   Water table

So, Do We Drink the Dirt?

Groundwater makes its way back to the surface through springs and wells. Springs are places where groundwater naturally seeps above ground. Wells are drilled or dug into the ground to tap into the aquifer. Once a well is drilled, a pump draws the water out. The pumps can be hand pumps or electric pumps, and they pump water out of wells from Africa to Alaska, and from India to Iowa. In the U.S., 290,000 million liters (76,500 million gallons) of water are pumped from the ground every day. That's four swimming pools of water for every person in our country!

Niagara Springs bursts out of the ground in Thousand Springs State Park, Idaho.

Like Batteries, Only Wetter

Aquifers would dry up fast if they weren't continuously being recharged—filled back up again. Rain soaking into soil or flowing down mountains recharges aquifers. Water in rivers and lakes can also seep into the ground and help recharge them. If recharging can't keep up with pumping, guess what? The water level in the aquifer drops—and eventually the well runs dry.

Being There

Well Grounded

Although Albuquerque, New Mexico, looks dry, there is water underneath this desert city. Ninety water wells tap into the Santa Fe Group Aquifer. Each well is almost 1 meter (3 feet) in diameter and as much as 518 meters (1,700 feet) deep. Together, they provide Albuquerque with over 114 billion liters (30 billion gallons) of water per year—that's enough to fill the Empire State Building more than 100 times. But how long can the city sponge off the groundwater? The water level in the aquifer has already dropped 55 meters (180 feet). If it drops much more, the ground above could start to sink. Uh-oh. Sinkholes.

Q Is for Quality

How good is groundwater? It can be fresh or a little salty. It can be clean or contaminated by chemicals. The chemicals could occur naturally in the rock, or they could be poured onto the ground by people. Examples? How about gasoline, pesticides, solvents, or other toxic chemicals from plastics or fuels. These chemicals can seep through soil from the surface just as water does, or they can leak out of landfills or buried storage tanks.

Water Loop-de-Loop

The amount of water on Earth has stayed about the same for millions of years. That's because water is constantly recycled. Earth's water cycle connects the water in the ocean, land, and air. A drop of water might fall as rain, and then soak into the soil and become groundwater. Tens or thousands of years later, the water may emerge as a spring and flow into a lake or stream. Then, as the air warms up, water molecules evaporate into the air, and the cycle begins again.

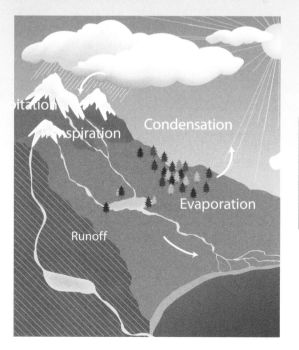

Precipitation

Transpiration

Condensation

Evaporation

Runoff

Water is always on the move—water vapor today, rain tomorrow, ice the day after.

4

GETTING WATER TO PEOPLE

Okay, so how does the water from lakes, rivers, or groundwater get to the people who need it? It depends on where they live. If the water doesn't come to the people, the people have to go to the water—and carry it home with them.

Too Far

In parts of Africa, women and children haul water long distances in big, heavy jugs—a tiring job that soaks up a lot of time and energy.

These Sudanese women balance jugs full of water as they walk the long road home.

4 U 2 Do

Weighty Job

Are you in shape for toting water? Imagine carrying drinking water to your family every day. Water weighs about 1 kilogram (2.2 pounds) per liter—water molecules are small, but heavy. Each member of your family needs 1.9 liters (eight 8-ounce glasses) of water each day. How many liters of water would you need for your family for one week? Forget baths, cooking, etc. Just calculate drinking water. How much would that weigh in kilograms? In pounds?

Check out your answers on page 40.

Pumping Water? Child's Play

So close, but. . . . What if clean water was underground, but there was no electricity to pump it? How about a pump that doubles as a merry-go-round? No electricity needed, just kid power! As kids play, they turn the merry-go-round. The merry-go-round works the pump, and water is pumped into a storage tank. There are 900 of these bringing fun and water to villages in Africa.

Well, Well

In many places, especially rural areas, every home has its own water well. These wells can be shallower than the wells that supply whole towns. Seventeen million(!) homes in the U.S. get their water from private wells.

All-Wheel Water

In some places fresh water may be scarce, far away, or contaminated. People may bring water to their homes by truck and store it in underground tanks called cisterns. They can collect rainwater and add to it.

Friends, Romans, and Aqueducts

What happens when a city's water supply is far away? Water can be pumped through pipes that are either underground or above ground. Aqueducts? They're structures that cleverly use gravity to guide water downhill—sometimes for hundreds of kilometers— to cities or homes that need it. The ancient Romans were famous for their beautiful, perfectly engineered aqueducts (below).

Wise Water Ways

As our world warms and our population climbs, fresh water becomes more and more of a prized resource. Drip by drop, people all over the globe are learning how to take better care of their water. Here are a few examples.

Siena, Italy

Even fancy hotels like this one in Siena, Italy are conserving water. Once-used water from this bathroom is piped to a marsh where it's naturally purified. Then the water's used to irrigate the hotel's fruit orchard and olive trees.

Las Vegas, Nevada

Residents are paid to rip up their water-sucking lawns and replace them with desert-adapted cacti, succulents, and drought-resistant shrubs.

Chungungo, Chile

It never rains in Chungungo, in Chile's Atacama Desert. But thick fog rolls in from the Pacific Ocean. Clever villagers trap water from the fog on nets, like spiderwebs catching mist. The collected water flows down a trough to a pipe to a reservoir about 6.4 kilometers (4 miles) away.

Gansu Province, China

In the 1990s, the Chinese government poured money into rainwater harvesting systems for homes in this poor, dry region. When it rains, rainwater is channeled to underground collection tanks. Now rainwater supplies almost 2 million people in Gansu Province with drinking water.

Sulaibaya, Kuwait

The world's largest water recovery plant is in the desert state of Kuwait. Wastewater is piped into the plant and purified to produce 378 million liters (100 million gallons) of clean water a day for factories and farms.

Ladakh, India

Clean drinking water gushes from this hand pump. The pump is connected to a school's water tank, which collects rainwater as it falls on the roof. Good news for girls living here—they can go to school instead of walking miles to pick up water for their family.

Perth, Australia

This desalination plant takes the salt out of seawater and provides 17 percent of the city of Perth's water. The process is powered by the wind—48 wind turbines make the electricity needed.

21

Watering the Big Apple

New York City uses 4.6 billion liters (1.2 billion gallons) of water every day. It all comes to town through a series of aqueducts from as far as 200 kilometers (125 miles) away. The water is stored in reservoirs outside New York City, and then sent into the city through three huge tunnels. They're cleverly named Tunnel Number 1, Tunnel Number 2 and, yes, Tunnel Number 3. The newest, Tunnel Number 3 (right), was started in 1970 and is still being built! When it is finally finished in 2020, it will span 97 kilometers (60 miles) and be 244 meters (800 feet) underground in some places. A 50-year project! That's tunnel vision.

The Main Thing

Did you know there's probably a system of pipes and valves hidden beneath your street? Almost all cities have municipal water systems. Once the water reaches the city by pipeline, it's stored in a reservoir or water tower. Then the water is sent to each neighborhood through big underground pipes called water mains. Smaller pipes carry the water from the mains into each home. Pumps push the water uphill; gravity pulls it downhill on its trip to the tap.

4 U 2 Do

Rainstorm Brainstorm

A water main broke so there's no water in your neighborhood. Now what? You're dirty, sweaty, and yucky from soccer. Then an idea hits you like lightning. There's a rainstorm coming. Is it possible to collect enough rainwater for a bath?

The U.S. Geological Survey says this: If it rains .8 centimeters ($\frac{1}{3}$ inch) in an area that's 3.6 meters by 3.6 meters or about 13 square meters, you could collect 114 liters (30 gallons) of water! That's enough for a bath. Now, say you used cake pans that are 20 centimeters x 20 centimeters to collect the water. How many pans will you need?

Check out your answers on page 40.

Keep It Clean

Water can carry a lot of things that you wouldn't want tumbling out of your tap. Before the water heads to your house, it goes through a treatment plant to flush out harmful things that hitch a ride on water— bacteria, viruses, heavy metals, pesticides, and other pollutants. Chlorine helps zap nasty microbes. Other chemicals clump together particles that can make water appear cloudy or taste funny. And intense filtering, through layers of sand and charcoal, sifts out other nasty stuff. By the time the water gets to your home, it's as pure as . . . water.

San Francisco's East Bay water treatment plant provides clean water to 1.3 million people.

Experts Tell Us
Kim Winton

Hydrologist
USGS Oklahoma Water Science Center

Kim Winton knows that groundwater is connected to rivers, lakes, and soil. And she knows that if toxic chemicals get into any of these, they can reach the groundwater. "People don't realize that groundwater is so easily contaminated," Kim says. "My job is to help protect groundwater . . . now and (for) the future." Her goal is to determine how deep groundwater is in a particular area, where it moves, and what things—like irrigation or underground gas tanks— might affect it.

Most large water wells in Oklahoma, where Kim works, tap into water about 100 to 250 meters (300 to 800 feet) below the surface. But someday, she says, we may need to tap into water that is much deeper. What if we contaminate that water now? "People take water for granted. There is no natural resource more precious than water," says Kim.

5

WANTED: CLEAN WATER

When you want a drink, you probably just go to the sink and turn on the faucet. But for many people around the world, getting clean water is not so easy.

Hard Water

Many of the things that we are doing are making it harder—not easier—to get clean water. In some cases, there isn't enough water for a growing population, or it's being diverted for uses other than drinking, or the available water is too dirty to be safe.

Too Little

In many places on Earth, there's just not enough water to go around. It happens all over, including in southwestern U.S. desert cities like Phoenix, Arizona (below), and Las Vegas, Nevada, which are among the fastest-growing cities in the country. And all those newcomers wash clothes, flush toilets, cook dinner, and water their yards.

Water Fight!

The Colorado River (right) might be your cup of tea. This long river flows through several thirsty states like Nevada, Arizona, and California. The states argue over it. Everyone—from lettuce farmers to power plant managers—wants a share of the water. Parks, golf courses, and homes compete for the water, too. So much water is drawn from the Colorado that the river runs dry before it reaches the ocean. Communities have to make tough choices about how they use their share of water. Maybe that golf course in the desert doesn't have to be so green.

Going Down, Down

Lake Chad in northern Africa is a freshwater lake that was once the size of Lake Erie. Because of a long drought in that part of the world, people and animals have to depend on the lake for water far more than they did before. The amount of water taken from the lake has quadrupled in the last 25 years. Today, Lake Chad is just a shadow of its former self—one-twentieth the size it was in the 1960s. Soon it may have to be renamed Pond Chad.

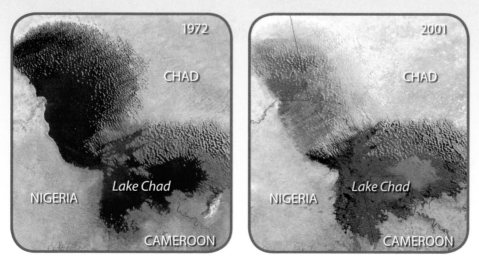

These satellite photos show that one of the world's great lakes is disappearing. North Africa's Lake Chad has shriveled to five percent of its former size.

The Incredible Shrinking Sea

Imagine walking out onto a pier and climbing into an old fishing boat that's docked there. But something's missing. The water! It's 64 kilometers (40 miles) away, and the boat is sitting on a dry, salt-crusted desert. Forty years ago, the waters of the Aral Sea lapped up against the pier. This sea in Uzbekistan was the fourth-largest inland sea in the world. But the rivers that fed it were diverted to irrigate cotton fields—a crop that doesn't grow naturally in this desert landscape. The result has been a disaster. Irrigation nearly sucked the rivers dry, and the sea began to shrink. And shrink. Much of what used to be the seafloor is now dry desert.

It's Natural . . .

33

As

Arsenic

74.922

But it's poison. Arsenic is a naturally occurring element that is found in many rocks and minerals in Earth's crust. It is a colorless, tasteless, odorless poison. If it seeps into groundwater, even low levels can cause big problems. Arsenic contamination is a major problem in West Bengal, India, where it is found in the deep groundwater used by nearly 100 million people. Not a welcome ingredient in drinking water.

Clean, Fresh Water for Everyone

No one can live without water. But what if the only water available is contaminated by sewage, animal waste, or garbage? Over 1 billion people live without access to clean, safe water. Many of them drink the dirty water anyway, because there's no choice. And many get sick. An estimated 2.2 million children, especially in Africa, India, and Bangladesh, die every year from illnesses caused by drinking dirty water.

Wake-Up Call

The Cuyahoga River in Ohio was so polluted that in November 1952, it actually caught fire (left). That caught people's attention. Imagine sending fire trucks to spray water on a fire *on* water! After that, people all over the U.S. became much more aware of the problems of water pollution.

6

CHANGING CLIMATE, CHANGING WATER

It started about 150 years ago. Temperatures on Earth began rising. The rise was so slow that it took scientists until the 1990s to be sure it was even happening. But they are sure. Earth is getting warmer. In fact, Earth's average temperature has warmed about 0.8°C (1.5°F) since about 1900.

Who, Us?

This climate change is caused by . . . us! How did we do that? We've changed our atmosphere by adding heat-trapping greenhouse gases—especially carbon dioxide—to the air. As we burn fossil fuels in our cars, factories, and power plants, they belch out carbon dioxide—lots of carbon dioxide.

Why the Worry?

Climate controls many aspects of our lives. One of the most important is water. It influences where water falls and whether it comes down as snow or rain. Climate is the reason some places, like western Washington state, are awash in water, and why other places, like Arizona, are as dry as yesterday's donut.

Weather Gone Wacko

Earth's climate is changing. And water resources around the world are feeling the heat. Glaciers are melting. Snow is turning into rain. Warmer air is sucking more water from oceans, lakes, rivers, plants, and soils. What goes up must come down—so more water is falling from the sky in intense storms. Some already wet places are getting even more rain—rain they don't need or want. Some dry regions are getting even less rain than they got before.

Grinnell Glacier in Glacier National Park, 1940 (top) and 2006 (bottom). Good-bye glacier, hello lake.

About Drought

If an area receives much less rainfall than normal for a long time, it's called a drought. Storm patterns, which bring rain, are influenced by ocean temperatures. And guess what influences ocean temperatures? A warming climate. Scientists say that the American Southwest is in for some extra-dry times. Most of the state of Arizona has had below-average rainfall since 1999. You're right. Below average for a desert is really, really dry.

Lake Mead, Nevada. The lake used to splash up on this fishing pier. Now the pier is suspended over the dry lake bed. The water in Lake Mead has dropped more than 30 meters (100 feet) since the 1960s.

Farm Futures?

A lot of the food in the U.S. is grown in the Midwest. But scientists aren't sure what may happen to river flows and groundwater in that part of the country. Back in the 1930s, a severe drought made things so tough for farmers that many packed up and left. Some scientists say that climate change could bring back similar conditions and again turn the Midwest into a Dust Bowl. Perhaps okay for a football game, but not for farming.

Squeeze Another Lemon

As our climate warms, you'll want extra lemonade. So will your plants. Well, maybe they'd prefer water—but you get the idea. In warmer weather, people and plants, animals and crops, all need more to drink. They need more water, not less! But hot weather has an effect on water use.

Turn Up the Air

Extra fans or air conditioning use extra electricity. That can mean more water running through hydroelectric dams, and more water circulating to cool electric plants. Did you know that some dams purposely generate extra electricity at about 5 PM, when people arrive home and try to cool their homes? Keep that water flowing.

Snow Going

When you see snowy mountains do you think of a big water tank? That's exactly how states in the western U.S. view the Rocky Mountains. But a warmer climate will cause more mountain snow to fall as rain. Rain doesn't stick around the way snow does. Farms in Colorado along the eastern edge of the Rockies depend on melting snow for irrigation in the late spring and summer. Uh-oh. Less snow melt, less sprinkler water.

A researcher with the Indian Institute of Himalayan Geology uses a chronometer to clock the flow of meltwater from glaciers.

Ice Was Nice

Glaciers around the world are melting—in the Andes in South America, the Alps in Europe, the Himalayas in Asia, and on Mount Kilimanjaro in Africa. People depend on these huge rivers of ice for a steady supply of water. Think of a glacier as a bank account. If its total amount of ice is how much we have in the bank, then the flow of melted water in the summer is like a withdrawal—it's available for people to use. How important are these glacial banks? The thousands of glaciers in the Himalayas feed more than a dozen major rivers and sustain a billion people downstream—that's one-sixth of the world's population!

First, Too Much . . .

Each summer, water from melting glaciers fills the rivers. More melting? More water—maybe too much water. If the water that drains into the river is more than it can hold—watch out! The river floods. In low-lying areas, this can swamp villages, roads, and farms. It can contaminate drinking water, ruin crops, and force people out of their homes. To make matters worse, floodwater isn't useful. Double whammy.

. . . Then, Too Little

Over time, as a glacier shrinks, the people downstream have the opposite problem. If the glacier disappears, there will be no water to feed the rivers. Farmers in Peru (right) depend on summer meltwater from high mountain glaciers in the Andes. But climate change is melting Peruvian glaciers into oblivion. Not good news for Peruvian potatoes or for the people who grow them for a living.

Here Comes the Sea

As water warms, it expands. As the oceans warm, seawater expands, too. That means the sea level rises. And that can be bad news for people living on beachfront property, but how could it affect our fresh water? As seas rise, the salt water can seep into groundwater and make it too salty to drink and too salty for irrigation.

These maps show Louisiana today (left) and how much of Louisiana would disappear (right) if the sea level rose one meter.

How Do They Know?

Modeling Job

Climate is complicated! It involves wind patterns, greenhouse gases, oceans, ice caps, and dozens of other factors. Computer models are mathematical models that simulate how these factors affect each other. Scientists change different variables, such as the amount of carbon dioxide, and then run the models over years to see what might happen under those conditions. Some models are so complicated that they take a month to run even on the world's biggest supercomputers.

Climatologist
Lamont Doherty Earth Observatory

Climatologist Richard Seager creates computer models of our climate to forecast changes. Even he is impressed by how well these models have correctly predicted complicated natural climates. Sometimes he finds something that explains an important event, like a drought. That really makes his work exciting. "It can be as good as finding an uncharted island," he says.

Richard and his colleagues have discovered that a warming climate is especially bad news for dry parts of the world like Mexico, the Mediterranean, and the southwestern U.S. Shifts in wind patterns will make these regions drier than ever. "Humans are changing the global climate in a way that is going to make life harder in these regions," says Richard. "These places need to begin now to plan for a future with less water in the streams and in the ground."

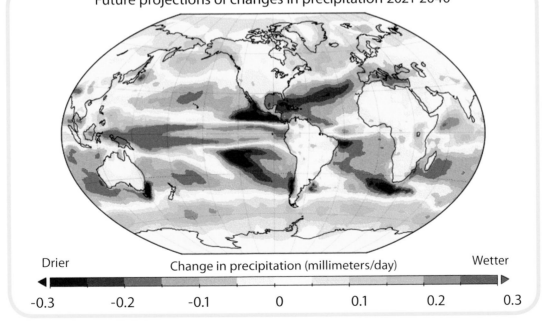

Future projections of changes in precipitation 2021-2040

Drier   Change in precipitation (millimeters/day)   Wetter

-0.3   -0.2   -0.1   0   0.1   0.2   0.3

7

DRY RUN

There are lots of things that people, companies, communities, and governments can do—and are doing—to make sure that everyone has access to clean, fresh water. Some solutions involve using less water, others make more water available, and still others purify dirty water.

Wheelbarrow + Water Barrel = Wheel Barrel!

In parts of Africa, villagers often live far from sources of clean water. They can spend hours a day carrying home buckets and jugs of water balanced on their heads. An invention called the Q-Drum is slowly changing that by putting water on the roll. The round, blue plastic drum is shaped like a thick doughnut. It holds a heavy 50 liters (13 gallons) of water, but even children can pull it, using a rope looped through its doughnut hole. That'll take a load off!

Drip Drip

How about using less water? Israel has no water to spare. Yet this dry nation grows so much produce that they have plenty of extra to export. Israeli farmers make every drop count, using drip irrigation instead of spray irrigation. In spray irrigation, up to 35 percent of the water evaporates or blows away in the wind. Drip irrigation uses pipes laid on the ground to drip just the right amount of water onto each plant. There's no waste and very little water lost to evaporation. Here, have an orange.

Cyber-Watering

Send your computer out to water the plants? No, but there are now computer-controlled watering systems that water plants very precisely—taking into account the weather, how deep the plants' roots are, and even where in the garden plants are. Smart watering like this saves lots and lots of water. No more sprinklers watering the lawn on rainy days.

Not Quite a Magic Wand, but . . .

A water treatment plant is usually a huge, complicated thing. But who says you can't take it with you? In recent years, companies have begun selling high-tech straws that you simply dunk in any pond, river, lake, or bog, and suck out a drink of clean water. What's the trick? The straws are tightly packed with filters, iodine beads, charcoal, and other things to purify water—no matter how dirty it is. They screen out dirt and kill bacteria and viruses. Backpackers and villagers around the world rely on the low-cost straws to make sure they always have a clean source of water at their fingertips.

Being There

Saving Lives with Old Clothes

In Bangladesh, contaminated water causes cholera epidemics among the poorest people. When people drink the water, they swallow tiny zooplankton that carry cholera bacteria. When the germ multiplies, it releases a toxin that causes diarrhea and cramping. Thousands and thousands of people get sick, and many die. American microbiologist Dr. Rita Colwell discovered that if water is filtered through four to ten layers of sari cloth—a fabric commonly used to make clothes—the germs are captured in its fine weave. And the number of cholera cases is cut in half!

Rita and her colleague gather water samples in Bangladesh.

Eric Mintz

Epidemiologist
Centers for Disease Control (CDC)

Before college, Eric Mintz (far left) traveled all over the world. He saw many people without access to clean water. Eric knows that drinking contaminated water kills millions of people every year from diseases like cholera and diarrhea. These diseases spread when raw sewage contaminates water sources.

As a doctor at the CDC, Eric is determined to make drinking water safer for more people. "To work, a solution has to be low-tech, cheap, and easy," he says. Eric's program saves lives by teaching people to add an inexpensive chemical to purify their water, and to store water in narrow-mouthed containers—containers that cleverly keep insects, animals, and people's dirty hands out of the water. "The long-term goal is for the rest of the world to have what you and I have—clean water to drink," he says.

Going Gray

After you wash an apple, how dirty is the water that goes down the drain? Lightly used water like this is called gray water. You may not want to drink it, but gray water can be recycled in many ways—for example, to flush the toilet. There are new systems that collect water from the sink, and then route it to the toilet. And gray water can be rerouted for other things, too—like watering a golf course or filling a pirate's lagoon. A pirate's lagoon? Yes, one hotel in Las Vegas recycles gray water from showers and uses it in their pirate show.

The Recycle Cycle

Drink recycled toilet water? You'd probably say, no way! The dusty, dry city of Windhoek, Namibia, (right) in Africa says "Why not." The city treats and purifies the wastewater. Then they treat it some more. Then some more. By the time treatment is done, the water is perfectly drinkable. Now, 30 percent of Windhoek's water comes from recycled wastewater. Other places are thinking about it, too, but many people find the idea of drinking wastewater tough to swallow.

UNSAFE WATER
DO NOT
SWIM, BATHE,
DRINK OR FISH

By order of
Middletown Dept. of
Health & Environment
One City Centre Plaza
Middletown OH and by
Ohio EPA 401 E. 5th St
Dayton OH 45402

The Big Fix

The Clean Water Act of 1977 helped make us nicer to our water and our water nicer to us. This U.S. government act made companies that pollute clean up their acts.

Rain, Rain, Come This Way

Ever heard rain pounding on the roof? Usually all that clean water goes to waste. Why not harvest it instead? As water runs off the roof, it goes through a filtering system that removes leaves, bacteria, and other things you don't want to drink. Then it's collected in a tank. The bigger the roof, the more rainwater there is. A rain collection system is being built in West Bengal, India, because the groundwater is contaminated by arsenic. This system will collect rainwater for 12 schools and give the students arsenic-free water to drink. Now *that* tastes better.

Big Glass of Ocean?

What if we could drink the oceans? Desalination takes the salt out of salt water. Desalination plants operate in dry spots like Saudi Arabia, Australia, Israel, and California. Some plants use a process called distillation—what you'd call boiling water! The boiling water creates steam. The steam is pure water vapor—it leaves the contaminants behind in the water. When the steam cools and condenses—presto, pure water. Another way to unsalt seawater is called reverse osmosis. A special filter separates tanks of salty and fresh water. Applying pressure to the salty side forces water through the filter but traps the clunky salt. Ah! Fresh water.

This desalination plant pumps out 29 million gallons of fresh drinking water each day for the island of Trinidad.

8

THINGS YOU CAN DO

Small steps make a big difference. Turn off the water when you brush your teeth, and you'll save 8 liters (2 gallons) or more of water every day. The tub is a water hog—the average shower uses 45 liters (12 gallons) less than a bath. Take showers instead of baths—hey, take shorter showers and you'll save even more. How easy is that?

Everything Plus the Kitchen Sink

Tap into some simple ideas for using less water in the kitchen. Dinnertime? Rinse the veggies in a bowl of water instead of washing each separately under the faucet. Cold drink sound good? Keep a water pitcher in the fridge instead of running the tap till the water gets cold. If you *do* run the water to get it hot or cold, catch it in a pot while you're waiting for it to reach the right temperature, and then use it later. Now you're really cooking!

Gone with the Wind

Do sprinklers around your home spray water into the air? If so, a lot of it's wasted—and not just because some of it might fall on the sidewalk. Some of it evaporates during its trip from the sprinkler to the lawn. Tell your family or your school about drip irrigation.

Being There

A True Story . . . About Us

Water use in the U.S. climbed steadily from the 1950s until it leveled off in about 1980. Then it actually decreased for a few years. Water use has stayed at about 1985 levels ever since! And all this time our population has been growing. This is good news. It shows we know how to conserve water, and that we care.

Waste Not, Want Not

As Earth's climate warms, the whole world is being challenged to provide everyone with clean, fresh water. How can we manage this bit of water magic? By trying harder. By inventing technologies that use water more efficiently, especially for irrigation. By passing laws that limit the amount of water that can be wasted. By doing the simple things that conserve water in our everyday lives. And, most importantly, by stopping the emission of greenhouse gases into the air. The great news is that, together, we

aquifer (n.) A soil or rock formation that contains enough water to use. (p. 15, 16)

climate (n.) Prevailing weather conditions for an ecosystem, including temperature, humidity, wind speed, cloud cover, and rainfall. (p. 4, 28, 33, 39)

desalination (n.) The process of removing salt from seawater to create drinkable fresh water. (p. 21, 37)

drought (n.) An extended period of unusually dry conditions. (p. 20, 25, 29, 33)

fossil fuel (n.) Nonrenewable energy resources such as coal, oil, and natural gas that are formed from the compression of plant and animal remains over hundreds of millions of years. (p. 28)

gray water (n.) Water that is lightly used, such as water used to shower or to rinse vegetables. (p. 36)

greenhouse gases (n.) Gases such as carbon dioxide, water vapor, and methane that absorb infrared radiation. When these gases are present in a planet's atmosphere, they absorb some of the heat trying to escape the planet instead of letting it pass through the atmosphere, resulting in a greenhouse effect. (p. 4, 28, 32, 39)

groundwater (n.) Water naturally contained in underground aquifers. (p. 12, 15, 16, 17, 23, 37)

irrigation (n.) The process of watering fields to supplement natural precipitation. (p. 23, 30, 32, 39)

pollutant (n.) A substance that is added to the environment (air, water, soil) and can lead to harmful effects for living organisms. (p. 4, 13, 27, 37)

reservoir (n.) A body of water created for water storage, often by damming a river. (p. 14, 15, 22)

Answers

4 U 2 Do, page 18
Family of 4— about 53 kilograms (117 pounds)
Family of 6— about 80 kilograms (176 pounds)

4 U 2 Do, page 22
324 pans